D1716491

To every Syracuse fan out there,
young and old.

Otto's ABC's

Requests for permission to make copies of any part of the work should be submitted online at info@mascotbooks.com or mailed to Mascot Books, 620 Herndon Parkway #320, Herndon, VA 20170.

PRT1017C

Printed in the United States

ISBN-13: 9781620861028
ISBN-10: 162086102X

www.mascotbooks.com

OTTO'S ABC'S

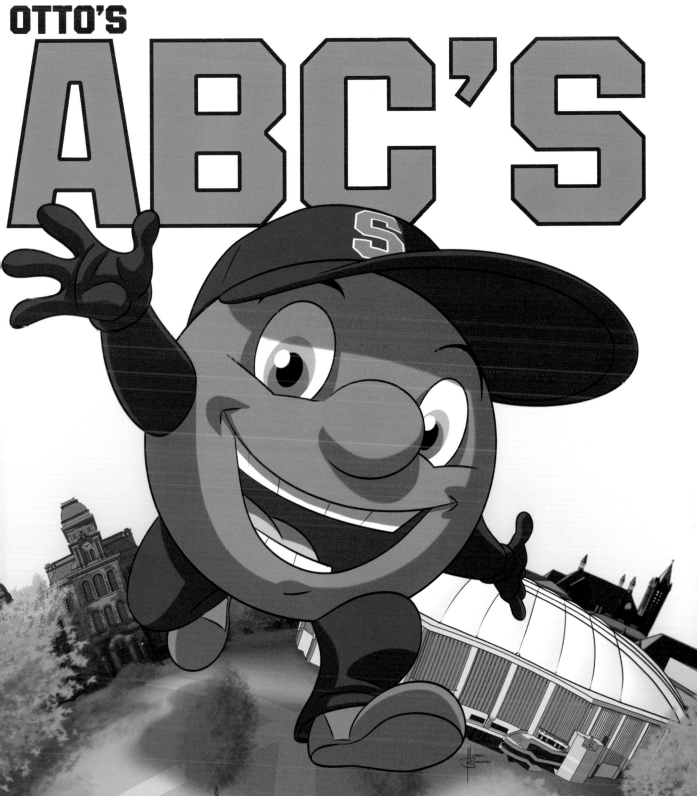

Kathryn Bradford, Kathleen Bradley and Leah Deyneka

Illustrated by Michael Borkowski

A is for ADMISSIONS

Where Otto welcomes you!

 is for **BOOKSTORE**

Where Otto reads and shops.

E is for ERNIE DAVIS

An amazing
athlete in
history.

F is for FORTY-FOUR

Otto's legendary number.

G
is for GRADUATION

When our alumni family grows.

H is for HALL OF LANGUAGES

See the clock up at the top?

I

is for INTERNATIONAL STUDENTS...

... who come from all around the World.

J is for JOIN

Otto belongs to many clubs on campus.

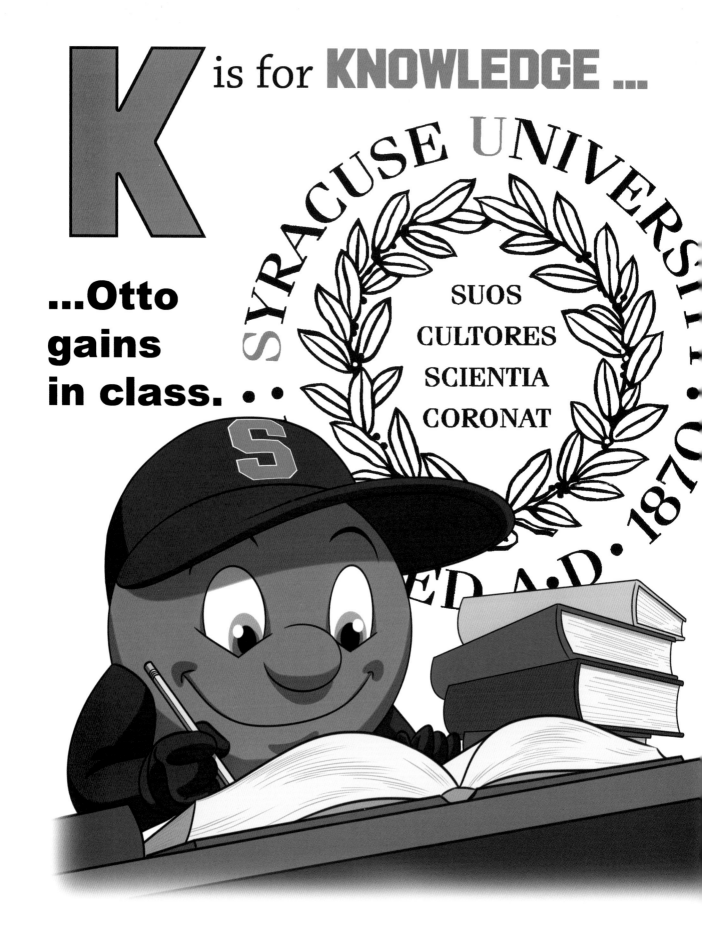

L

is for **LIBRARIES**

Where Otto studies.

M is for MARSHALL STREET

Where Otto meets his friends.

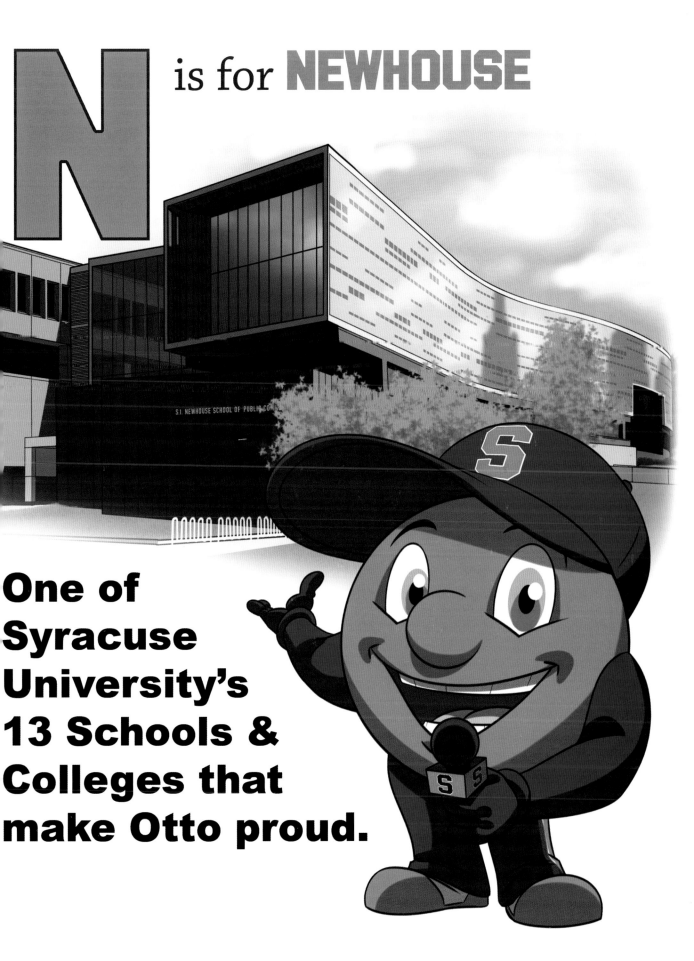

N is for NEWHOUSE

One of Syracuse University's 13 Schools & Colleges that make Otto proud.

O is for **ORANGE**

Otto's favorite color!

P is for PAN AM WALL OF REMEMBRANCE...

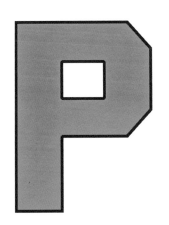

... where Otto pays tribute.

Q is for QUAD

A very busy place.

R is for **REAL...** MEN, WOMEN, ALUMNI, CHAMPIONS, DADS, FANS, GIRLS, MOMS, BOYS, GRANDPARENTS, KIDS... WEAR ORANGE!

S is for SYRACUSE

The city where Otto lives.

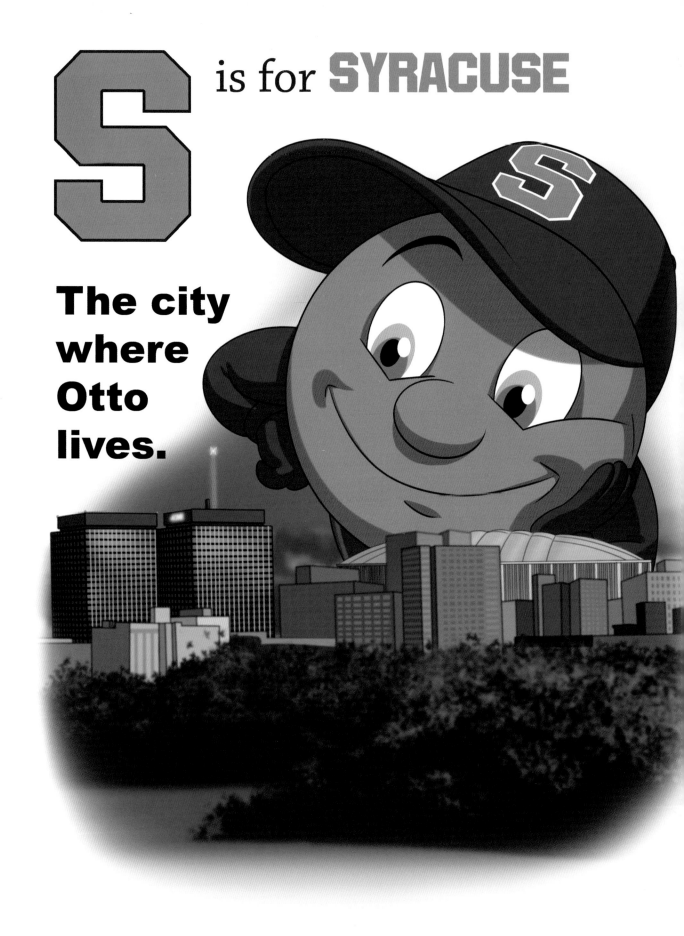

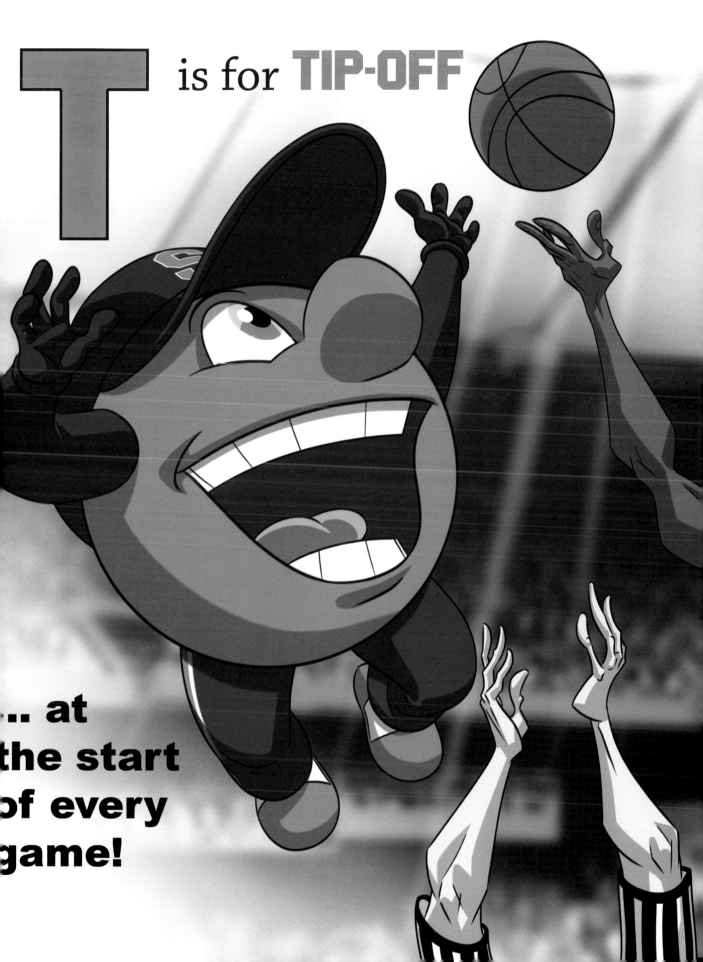

U is for **UNIFORMS**

Otto loves SU Sports!

V is for VETERANS

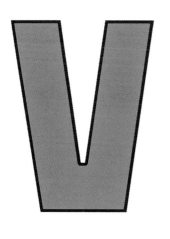

...who Otto honors every day.

W is for WINTER

...when Otto wears a coat, hat, boots, and mittens.

X is for **XYLOPHONE**

When Otto plays music with the band.

Y is for **YEAR 1870**

When Otto's school was built.